YOU CAN DO IT !

SO-AXY-801

Things You Can Do To
APPRECIATE
SCIENCE AND
LOVE THE
BIBLE

CHARLES ST-ONGE

CONCORDIA PUBLISHING HOUSE · SAINT LOUIS

This book is dedicated to my daughters, Olivia and Sophia.

May they continue to grow in their appreciation of their world and in their love for the Lord who created it.

Copyright © 2013 Concordia Publishing House
3558 S. Jefferson Ave., St. Louis, MO 63118-3968
1-800-325-3040 · www.cph.org

The quotations from the Lutheran Confessions are from *Concordia: The Lutheran Confessions*, second edition; edited by Paul McCain, et al., copyright © 2006 Concordia Publishing House. All rights reserved.

Scripture quotations are from the ESV Bible® (The Holy Bible, English Standard Version®), copyright © 2001 by Crossway Bibles, a publishing ministry of Good News Publishers. Used by permission. All rights reserved.

Catechism quotations are taken from *Luther's Small Catechism with Explanation*, copyright © 1986, 1991 Concordia Publishing House. All rights reserved.

Manufactured in the United States of America

1 2 3 4 5 6 7 8 9 10   22 21 20 19 18 17 16 15 14 13

INTRODUCTION

I have always loved science and engineering.
My first love, after Jesus and my parents, was my Lego® set. I distinctly remember my father teaching me to alternate rows of blocks to build a stable wall, a real improvement over my parallel, non-overlapping columns. When I was a child, my books were about space travel, electricity, and world atlases. I still have my book on spaceflight and anxiously await the day when my two daughters will be interested in pouring over it with me. Now, at bookstores, I'm more likely to pick up *Popular Science* than the latest novel. We go to our county park to launch model rockets. I build my own computers. My wife knows it, my kids know it, and my congregation knows it: I am a science geek.

Rev. Paul Schult, who taught my catechism class at Trinity Lutheran in Sudbury, Canada, scribbled on one of my tests that I should consider entering the public ministry. In my last year of high school, when I was deciding about college, I asked Pastor Schult what I should do. He reaffirmed that he thought I was "pastor material." He said that if the Lord wanted me to be a pastor, then I wouldn't be happy doing anything else. Turns out he was right. Then he said, "but try something else first." To the surprise of my high school English and history teachers, but not my math and science teachers, I left home to study civil engineering at the University of Waterloo in Waterloo, Canada.

I didn't have a problem integrating my faith with science until university, but what happened to me then is not what you might think. You see, I grew up in a church body that has no difficulty accepting the prevailing scientific wisdom even when it conflicts with clear scriptural teachings. I grew up believing that the universe began more than a dozen billions of years ago in the explosion of a singularity. Over the subsequent billions of years, matter coalesced into the galaxies, stars, and star systems we see today. Several hundreds of millions of years ago, life on earth arose from previous inorganic matter. Over time, under the pressure of the environment working on random genetic mutations, life as we know it evolved on earth—and possibly elsewhere. Who knows how many intelligent races fill our universe, waiting for us to make contact?

But at college, I ran into a very different breed of Christian. These "evangelicals" believed that much of the conventional, scientific wisdom was simply wrong—wrong because it conflicted with God's revealed Word in the Bible. These Christians rejected what I believed were clear teachings of science in favor of a book that to me didn't say much about science. I thought that the Bible was about faith in the world yet to come, while science was about the here and now! But after a particular engineering geology class, a classmate admitted that he didn't accept that the earth was 4.5 billion years old. He didn't believe that all species on earth evolved through common descent from a first organism that arose naturally from nonlife. He pointed out to me that Genesis 1 and 2 give a radically different explanation for the advent of life. I remember shrugging and admitting that I was much less interested in the details of the Genesis creation story than in the data of the best researchers. *God did it*, I thought; isn't it enough to simply believe that? Couldn't God have used evolution to bring about life on earth? Wasn't the big bang a pretty close approximation to the Lord's first recorded words, "Let there be light"?

I completed my bachelor's degree in engineering and then a master's of science degree at Queen's University. I ended up working for a large American consulting firm in Washington DC. But the questions raised by my friend in college stayed with me. I realized that I was a small part of the great worldview debate of our time. That debate can be encapsulated in one simple question: are the Scriptures or humanity's theorems and models the final word on truth?

I have since rejected the models and hypotheses of evolutionary theory on both biblical and scientific grounds. I have also rejected, on biblical grounds, an old age for the earth (even the science on this point is ambiguous). In both cases, the Spirit of the Lord has brought me under His tutelage, rather than allowing me to keep trying to put God under mine. I have come to appreciate Luther's words in the Small Catechism: "I believe that I cannot by my own reason or strength believe in Jesus Christ, my Lord, or come to Him; but the Holy Spirit has called me by the Gospel" (Third Article).

This book, *5 Things You Can Do to Appreciate Science and Love the Bible*, is written for Christians who, like me, love science but also love their Lord and the revelation He gives of Himself and of history in the Holy Scriptures. This is a book for those who know that God gives humans great intelligence to interpret what we see around us and a great curiosity to do so. It is also for those who recognize that we are a fallen race that can still be deceived by the devil, a "liar and the father of lies" (John 8:44). It is a book for those who want to be faithful to God in a world dominated by scientism, a world where God no longer seems to have a place. This is a practical book, meant to encourage us to take action to strengthen our faith, the faith of our children, and that of our congregations. It is a challenging book, meant to guide our discussions in areas that too often go undiscussed. Most important, it is a book meant to glorify our great God and Savior, Jesus Christ, through whom heaven and earth exist.

There is a famous quote often attributed to Satchel Paige or to Mark Twain: "It's not what you don't know that'll hurt you. It's what you know that just ain't so." Nothing could be truer when it comes to matters of science and Christianity. Much of the supposed conflict between God's revelation in the Bible and our understanding of the universe through observation is a matter of presuppositions, or of believing things that aren't necessarily so.

Suppose I enter my house after having been out for a few hours. I'm horrified to discover that my books have been thrown all over the floor, my TV has been turned over, and my clothes pulled out of my dresser. All that's still in place are the walls, ceiling, and floor. I immediately think, *Vengeful ghosts. There's no other explanation.*

But other possibilities might go through your mind. If you know I live in Houston, and you know how serious the problem of crime is in major urban areas, you might suspect this is the work of burglars. That it might have been ghosts probably didn't cross your mind. Both of us were working off the same set of data: a ransacked house. But after observing that data, we drew different conclusions. Why?

Our explanations for things that happen are significantly influenced by our mental environment and by our worldview. A mental environment is a set of presuppositions that everyone in a culture or society works from. A worldview is a personal or corporate commitment to a certain set of pre-suppositions. Some worldviews flow naturally from a mental environment. Some clash. We can choose our worldview, but not our mental environment.

The Christian worldview accepts the Scriptures as the Word of God. The Bible does not merely contain the Word of God; the Holy Spirit has spoken through the prophets, apostles, and evangelists in such a way that we are hearing not their thoughts but the thoughts of our Lord Himself. To understand the world and our place in it, Christians turn first to the Bible.

The non-Christian worldview is either modernist or postmodernist. Modernists accept some core principles through which they interpret the world and believe everyone else should accept the same core principles. Post-modernists may or may not have a set of core principles and are not convinced that their principles need to be held by anyone else.

Christians and non-Christians live in the same mental environment. That mental environment is one in which science reigns supreme. Scientific proof is the only evidence that counts. To win an argument in a mental environment like ours, quote a researcher, university laboratory, or think tank that supports your position.

How do we take our Christian worldview, which accepts the Bible as the final word on truth, out into a world where scientific study is the final word? We must

• be certain of our own worldview;

- know how to live with our worldview in our mental environment;
- understand how our worldview shapes our interpretation of facts; and
- know how to use our God-given intellect and our Spirit-restored reason to interpret the facts in light of Scripture.

Know Your Worldview

Why do we believe the Bible is the Word of God, and what do we mean when we say this? Can you explain why the Scriptures shape your personal worldview? Do you always interpret the world through the lens of God's revelation? Can you show others that the Bible can be trusted as the Word of God? Peter wrote that Christians should be "prepared to make a defense to anyone who asks you for a reason for the hope that is in you . . . with gentleness and respect" (1 Peter 3:15). Knowing your own worldview is an important place to start.

Jesus claimed to be the very Son of God. He claimed that He was the definitive revelation of who God is and what He is truly like. Jesus demonstrated the kind of relationship God wants with us by His own life and death. He backed up His teachings with signs and wonders. These signs, which we often refer to as "miracles," point to Jesus' reliability as a communicator of truths about

Learn your own worldview so you can interpret facts consistent with it.

the world. In the Book of Job, God asks where Job was when the world was made (38:4). The answer is that only one being was there: God! So God is the only one who can give an accurate report of what happened at creation. Jesus' miracles, especially His resurrection, attested to by numerous eyewitnesses, confirmed that He could speak authoritatively about all these things.

Throughout His ministry, Jesus confirmed the authority of the Hebrew Scriptures, which we now call the Old Testament:

- He used the account of the creation of Adam and Eve to justify marriage as the union of one man and one woman for life (Mark 10:6–9).

- He accepted the account of Jonah's three days and three nights in the belly of a great fish (Matthew 12:40).

- He accepted all of the Old Testament as the actual words of God—words about Jesus Himself (Luke 24:44).

Therefore, we, too, can accept the words of the Hebrew prophets and of Moses as the authoritative Word of God Himself.

In Matthew 10, Jesus warned His disciples about the future, but then also made an astonishing promise:

Beware of men, for they will deliver you over
to courts and flog you in their synagogues,

and you will be dragged before governors and kings for My sake, to bear witness before them and the Gentiles. When they deliver you over, do not be anxious how you are to speak or what you are to say, for what you are to say will be given to you in that hour. *For it is not you who speak, but the Spirit of your Father speaking through you.* (vv. 17–20, emphasis added)

Jesus is stating that when His apostles, who traveled with Him from the beginning of His ministry, gave a witness to the Gospel, it was God Himself speaking through them. God inspired their words. So today, when we read the records of the apostles' teachings contained in the New Testament, we are reading what God wants us to know about

- Himself;

- Jesus;

- our world's origin and destiny; and

- salvation.

The words of the apostles, like Jesus' words and the words in the Old Testament, are the Word of our God Himself.

To interpret the facts of our world correctly, the Scriptures should shape our worldview. God's Word gives us everything we need to correctly understand the things we observe in the world.

Learn How Worldviews Affect Data Interpretation

We've all received e-mails or messages that seemed a little fishy. One of my colleagues in ministry is a pastor from Nigeria who is currently teaching in his homeland. I often ask him if he's ever met one of the countless Nigerians who have inherited millions of dollars but needs an American to help him access it. He says no. The Web site snopes.com is dedicated to sorting truth from fiction on the Internet. Yet how often do we believe without a second thought e-mails that include statements by "prominent scientists" or declare the results of an "extensive study"?

As you read earlier, our interpretation of data depends on our presuppositions. A presupposition is something we accept as true. Scientists rarely start with an open-ended question, study data, then come to an unexpected conclusion. In fact, the scientific process demands that they have an idea of what might happen in an experiment. The first step in the standard scientific process is the formation of a hypothesis.

When a scientific "fact" seems to conflict with your worldview, ask what the presuppositions were in determining that fact.

Proving or disproving that hypothesis can have consequences to a scientist's livelihood. The right answer can bring thousands, even millions, of grant money. The wrong answer can bring job loss. Although we would all like to believe that scientists remain objective, the truth is that they often feel tremendous pressure to have the results of their studies or experiments go a certain way.

The Scriptures tell us that all humans are born with a tendency toward presupposition against belief in God. The Augsburg Confession states it plainly: "since the fall of Adam [Romans 5:12], all who are naturally born are born with sin [Psalm 51:5], that is, without the fear of God, without trust in God" (II 1). Is it any wonder, then, that non-Christian scientists are biased against finding evidence of a Creator? If scientists can be biased by mundane things like money or power, how much more can they be biased by their own sinful nature?

Every scientist considers scientific problems through the lens of his or her worldview, Christian or otherwise. This is especially true when we leave the realm of things we can observe and enter the realm of things that happened in the past, that may happen in the future, or that are beyond the range of our microscopes and telescopes. These are things we cannot observe directly, so we must infer what happened or is happening based on what we can observe.

Consider predictions about future events. No one has been to the future, so it cannot be observed scientifically. But based on past events that have been observed, we can apply scientific models to predict what might happen in the future. Such predictions are always tentative. The further into the future we try to predict, the less accurate our predictions can become. This is especially true as we account for a lot of variables, as weather and climate forecasters must do.

The same is true of our understanding of the past. The fossils, rocks, stars, and cells we examine today can be studied scientifically to determine their composition right now. We can guess where they came from, but we cannot make statements with the same scientific accuracy as when we talk about what we see right now.

All scientific data about the world exists now, in the present. To make estimates about the past and predict the future, we must do what scientists call "extrapolating beyond the data set." Again, we draw lines from the present into the past and into the future, lines that become less and less certain the farther from the present we go and the more complicated the event we consider. It is when we must guess about the past and predict the future that our biases really come into play.

As Christians, we pray that the Spirit would make God's Word our worldview. We want the truths communicated by our Lord, the Alpha and Omega, to shape how we interpret the facts we see in our world. Here are some worldviews that cause non-Christian scientists to paint a history and future of the world that is often at odds with God's revealed Word.

Learn about the presuppositions that can lead scientists in a particular direction.

1. ***Naturalistic materialism:*** the late American scientist Carl Sagan popularized through television and in books the idea that there is nothing beyond the physical universe that we can directly observe. If it was not made

up of matter or energy, Sagan believed it just wasn't worth studying. This bias or worldview is known as naturalistic materialism. This worldview rules out any observable supernatural intervention in the affairs of the cosmos. Naturalistic materialists argue that since matter and energy generally obey set natural laws, then everything in the universe, including its origin, can be explained by matter and energy following those set natural laws.

In recent decades, some scientists have recognized a third component of the universe that is distinct from matter and energy: information. The DNA within living organisms, for example, contains the information needed to replicate and build the structures within the organism itself. Naturalistic materialists believe that natural selection acting on random genetic mutations is a sufficient mechanism to explain the rise of DNA information within plants and animals.

While Einstein's work on relativity, the famous $E=mc^2$, demonstrated the equivalency of matter and energy, it did not demonstrate how matter and energy can, by themselves, give rise to information. No scientific theory has done that. Information comes, as far as we know it, from intelligence alone. Design implies a designer. The existence of DNA information is a serious problem for naturalistic materialism.

2. **Atheism:** While not all naturalistic materialists are atheists, all atheists are naturalistic materialists. Atheism adds another level of bias to the naturalistic materialist worldview. A naturalistic materialist may say that God could exist but

that we cannot observe signs of His existence through scientific observation. However, an atheist has predetermined that it is not possible to find such evidence because God does not exist.

One of the arguments atheists make against belief in a supernatural creator is that such a belief is a mere crutch. Theologian Alister McGrath says we could just as easily say that the inverse is also true, that atheists disbelieve to avoid ultimate judgment for their actions. Many people believe that science has disproved God's existence. But the truth is that many scientists conduct their work as if they are atheists, so their bias affects how they interpret the evidence. Like a drug manufacturer that has a vested interest in showing that their chemical is safe, atheists have a vested interest in interpreting data to fit their worldview.

3. *Escalating commitment:* In the 1970s, social scientist Barry Staw identified a phenomenon he called the fallacy of escalating commitment. What he saw was that some people continue doing something that has had terrible results in the hope that a different result is just around the corner. The more committed people are to a certain course of action, the more likely they are to stick with it even if it isn't working.

Many scientists are committed to certain models and theories even as evidence mounts against them. This is one of the reasons why scientists have stuck with the model of neo-Darwinian evolution as an explanation for the rise of different kinds of life on earth. There is no other plausible theory conforming to naturalistic materialism. If you are a naturalistic materialist, and certainly if you are an atheist, evolution is the only show in town. Commitment to the theory is so great that few recognize the theory's difficulties. This is related to physicist Thomas Kuhn's idea of a "paradigm shift," and how difficult it is for the scientific community to accept new ideas.

Because of this reluctance to give up a model or theory, it is possible for almost everyone in the scientific community to be wrong about a certain idea. The late Michael Crichton, famous doctor and science fiction writer, pointed this out in a lecture at the California Institute of Technology. He reminded his audience that science, unlike politics, is not about consensus; science is about getting things right.

Christians are accused of interpreting the data we observe in the world to fit our presuppositions. Guilty as charged! But we aren't the only ones who are guilty. Everyone tends to interpret data to fit their worldview. Whether you approach the universe as having been created by a good God who reveals Himself or as an accidental product of a purposeless explosion following natural laws that came into existence by themselves, you are interpreting facts to fit your worldview.

Interpreting Facts
through the Lens of Our Worldview

As Christians, we believe that God is daily renewing our minds by the Holy Spirit, who speaks to us through the Scriptures. We are being conformed to the image of Christ in the way we think and the way we act. Certainly our Old Adam and Satan would like nothing better than to give us false knowledge. But to the extent that we remain faithful to God's Word, we can rightly interpret the world. Let's consider some practical examples of letting God's Word direct our thinking.

1. **Evolution**: Charles Darwin, an amateur scientist, popularized an idea that had been taking shape in the nineteenth century: that animals change through adaptation to their environment. The modern concept of neo-Darwinism is not Darwinism, strictly speaking, but the concept that all life is descended from some original simple life form through natural selection acting on random genetic mutations. Neo-Darwinism does not try to explain where that first life came from (that particular science is known as abiogenesis, or the origin of life from nonlife).

Neo-Darwinist theory is a classic example of using data observed in the present to make educated guesses about the past. We observe natural selection in the present. Humans breed animals, such as dogs and horses, to get breeds with certain characteristics (e.g., taller dogs or faster horses). Neo-Darwinian theory takes this natural selection and extrapolates it back in time to something we have never observed: natural selection giving rise to new genetic information. Author Ken Ham points out that at the London Museum of Natural History's exhibit on evolution, the exhibit on weasels contains this caption: "When weasels breed together, they produce more weasels, just like themselves." That is what we have observed in nature. The weasels may adapt to their environment, but we have not observed them adapting into another form of life based on different genetic information.

The Scriptures tell us that in the beginning God created all plants and animals according to their kinds (Genesis 1:11, 21, 24). He did not say He created every form of dog that we see today, some of which have only come into existence recently through breeding. But He did create every kind. Using science, we can see that our scriptural bias that kinds stay kinds seems to hold. The bias that all kinds of life came about through natural selection acting on the random mutation of one kind has not been seen to happen; it is conjecture designed to fit with the preconceived bias of neo-Darwinism.

2. *Big bang:* A second idea concerning history held by many scientists, especially those inclined to atheism and naturalistic materialism, is the big bang. The concept that the entire universe began from a single singularity arose because of astronomical observations in the mid-twentieth century. Before that, most scientists believed that the universe had always existed pretty much as we see it today. But the observations of Edwin Hubble provided evidence that the stars and galaxy we observe are moving away from each other. At first it looked like the earth might be the center of the whole universe, since everything seems to be moving away from us. But some be-

Visit the Answers in Genesis Creation Museum in Northern Kentucky for an alternate scientific explanation of the origin of life biased toward God's Word.

lieve that it is the universe itself which is expanding. Think about a deflated balloon with black marker points drawn on it. The dots are all fairly close to each other because the balloon is small. But if you blow air into the balloon, it gets bigger and all the points move away from one another. This led some scientists to suggest that if the entire universe were expanding, then there might have been some point in the past when it was infinitely small.

The big bang theory uses data we observe in the present—the movement of stars and galaxies away from one another—to make educated guesses about the past. If we do not believe we have a revealed word from the creator of the universe about how all this happened, or if we are biased toward an explanation that does not imply or require a creator, we will do our best to come up with a theory that requires no creator. The big bang is that theory.

Like neo-Darwinism, however, the big bang theory also has shortcomings that suggest it is an inadequate scientific explanation. For example, we don't see the kinds of stars that the theory predicts should dot the galaxies of the universe. The constant background temperature of the universe requires an uneven expansion of the universe, an expansion that was fast, then slow, then fast again.

Read about Dr. Jason Lisle, the head of the Institute for Creation Research, who has a PhD in astrophysics from the University of Colorado. For starters, check out http://www.answersingenesis.org/home/area/bios/j_lisle.asp.

The distant galaxies we can observe reveal a fully formed structure, not a developing structure that the big bang theory predicts. But like evolution, the big bang is the only theory for the universe's origin that naturalistic materialists have.

For those of us who believe the Lord created the heavens and the earth and revealed their creation in His Word, we don't have to rely on the big bang. We have holy knowledge from the One who made it happen. We can examine the same stars, galaxies, and physics of the universe that non-Christians see and confidently say they point to a God who delights in beauty and elegance. We can look at the universe with our own eyes and through the eyes of scientific instruments and declare with David, "the heavens declare the glory of God, and the sky above proclaims His handiwork" (Psalm 19:1).

Some Things to Remember when Reading "Science" Stuff

There are lots of scientists, some of them Christian, some of them not, who know it's important to read all science articles critically. One group, the American Institute for Technology and Science Education (www.aitse.org), has produced a document listing ten ways to test scientific articles for truth and exaggeration. Here are three:

1. Does the article claim that something is proven or is a fact? If it's a fact, no scientist would waste words saying so. Scientists can rarely prove something. Ken Ham, the head of Answers in Genesis, is careful to point out that

we cannot disprove the concept of evolution anymore than we can prove the Bible is God's Word. What we can do is find evidence that, until or unless it is contradicted, supports a given theory or model.

2.   Can the claims of the article be measured? Science observes things, counts them, and summarizes what has been observed and counted. If an article claims that all Muslims secretly wish they were Christians, how can that be observed or measured? If it's a secret desire, how was it discovered in every Muslim on earth?

3.   Is the research based on unproven assumptions or extrapolations? An example of an unproven assumption is that life arises naturally out of nonlife. As I mentioned above, science currently has no robust explanation for how this could have happened. We have never observed it happening. The process of pasteurization developed by Louis Pasteur, which enables us to purify food products, assumes that life cannot arise from nonlife under general conditions in short periods of time. An example of an extrapolation is taking things we know to be true and developing them to an extreme. For example, if we can breed a dog that is twice as big as the original dog we started with, we might extrapolate that we could eventually breed a dog that is more than a mile high. That extrapolation fails to take into account food supply, limitations of skeletal structure, and many other considerations.

Final Thoughts

Take to heart Michael Crichton's reminder that a majority of scientists can be wrong. No one knew until Einstein that nothing could travel faster than light. No one knew until the experiments of the early twentieth century that particles like photons behave like matter and energy. No one knew until just recently that our entire DNA, not just our genes, performs critical functions. If you see a scientific statement that seems to contradict the Scriptures, do some research! Someone, somewhere, has probably written about the problem and can point to an answer.

Key Points

- We interpret facts through the lens of our mental environment and our worldview. Christians want our scriptural worldview to shape our perceptions while recognizing that we live in a Western, "scientific" mental environment.

- Our society's worldview has become less Christian and no longer accepts that there is a God who has revealed Himself to us in His Word. Many scientific models and theories, therefore, assume there is no God while attempting to explain what we observe.

- What we observe in the world does not directly contradict anything we read in Holy Scripture. Contradictions come from the models based on nonscriptural starting points.

- Christians with a nonscience background can use basic principles to interpret the world in line with Scripture and to discern when they are reading something that is not a "fact" but simply one possible interpretation of the data.

Discussion Questions

1. Think about a scientific fact that seems to conflict with Scripture. Is it an actual fact or an interpretation of a fact? What presuppositions went into the interpretation? What presuppositions should a Christian use to interpret the fact?

2. What aspect of science or our modern worldview causes your faith to stumble the most? Why does it seem to go against Scripture? Have you asked someone knowledgeable on the topic if anyone else has asked the same question and resolved it?

Action Items

1. Ask your pastor to lead a Bible study on what the Scriptures say about themselves. Have him teach how to explain to a non-Christian that the Scriptures can be trusted as the Word of God.

2. Start a library in your church, or add to your existing church library. Include books that deal with science from a Christian worldview perspective. Some books to consider:

Werner Gitt, *In the Beginning was Information* (Master Books, 2006)

Ken Ham, *The New Answers Book 1, 2, and 3* (Master Books, 2011)

Joel Heck, *In the Beginning, God: Creation from God's Perspective* (Concordia, 2011)

Stephen Meyer, *Signature in the Cell* (HarperOne, 2009)

Various authors, Faith on the Edge series (Concordia, 2001–2005)

3. Arrange for a Christian scientist to speak in your congregation or area. Invite your friends and neighbors.

Earlier, we learned some basic principles for thinking about the world scientifically as people who believe God reveals Himself to us in His Word and in that Word become flesh, Jesus Christ. Let's think now about a very important group of Christians who need to know these principles: children. If there was one group of people who had a special place in Jesus' heart, it was infants and little kids: "And He took a child and put him in the midst of them, and taking him in His arms, He said to them, 'Whoever receives one such child in My name receives Me, and whoever receives Me, receives not Me but Him who sent Me' " (Mark 9:36–37).

Notice a few things about this passage. First, Jesus does not merely point to a random child and say, "Be nice to kids like that!" No, He takes the child up in His arms—hugs him!—and demonstrates that receiving children isn't just talking about them but interacting with them. In the next chapter of Mark, Jesus brings home the point again: "Let the children come to Me; do not hinder them, for to such belongs the kingdom of God. Truly, I say to you, whoever does not receive the kingdom of God like a child shall not enter it" (10:14–15).

What does He do next? "And He took them in His arms and blessed them, laying His hands on them" (v. 16). There is simply no getting around it; ministering to children by caring for them body and soul should be a primary concern of the Church. This idea isn't limited to the New Testament either.

The Book of Deuteronomy was Moses' last major sermon to the people of Israel. As the people were about to enter the land of Canaan, Moses gave them the great creed of the Old Testament along with these instructions:

> Hear, O Israel: The Lord our God, the Lord is one. You shall love the Lord your God with all your heart and with all your soul and with all your might. And these words that I command you today shall be on your heart. You shall teach them diligently to your children, and shall talk of them when you sit in your house, and when you walk by the way, and when you lie down, and when you rise. (6:4–8)

One of our primary responsibilities as congregations and as Christian adults is to instill in children a love for God's Word and a trust that it will give them the tools they need to interpret their lives and their world. As they grow up, children are confronted with more and more questions:

- How should I act toward others?
- Whom should I obey: parents? teachers? friends? society? the Church?
- Where did I come from?
- Why am I here?
- What should I do with my life?
- What is the purpose of life? (Is there a purpose?)

Sinful humanity has long sought and found answers to these questions far from God's Word. For a while, though, the

Western world's answers were the Scriptures' answers. The great cathedrals of Europe and the proliferation of churches in America testify that for a short time, historically speaking, our society was Christian. This is no longer the case. Although a majority of people in the United States claim to be Christian, their worldview is certainly not. These self-professed Christians no longer define marriage as the Bible defines it (a majority of Americans support gay and lesbian marriage). As a pastor, it is increasingly rare that I meet a couple that wants me to marry them and is not already "married"—that is, living together. An increasing number of Christians have no problem with early term abortion. Many view theft of intellectual or creative property—music, books, movies—as acceptable.

Never before has it been so important to teach our children the scriptural view of the world and to give them reasons to trust the Word of God.

Why This Topic Is Critical

For many, educating children has consisted mostly in telling them basic stories of the Bible. Our kids know that God created the world, sent a flood, and called Abraham and Sarah to go to the Promised Land. They've heard about Joseph and his multicolored coat, about David and his slingshot, and about Jesus and His miracles. What we've often taught our kids is simply that: a collection of stories. Those stories compete against all the other stories our kids will hear, stories such as these:

• A group of Jedi fight for freedom against an evil empire.

• A mermaid becomes a princess.

• Animal friends survive an ice age.

• A teen becomes a warrior to fight for her family.

• A teen becomes a vampire to start a family.

Bible stories too often get lost among the world's stories.

But, you say, our Bible stories really happened! Of course they did, and that's what makes them so important. However, do we teach them as if they were history or as if they belong in the same category as stories that begin "a long time ago, in a galaxy far, far, away"? A New Testament professor at a West Coast university found that only 23 percent of his students, 95 percent of whom called themselves Christian, could properly sequence these key events from Israel's history:

a) The Israelites enter the Promised Land.

b) Judah goes into exile.

c) Israel is divided into two kingdoms.

d) David is made king.

Use a Bible, such as *The Lutheran Study Bible*, that has a history timeline that connects biblical events to world history. When you read a story with your kids, tell them when it happened in history.

(The correct sequence is a, d, c, and b.) The majority of those students claimed to love the Scriptures, but they learned the Bible as a bunch of stories that didn't clearly relate to each other. And if they could not relate one Bible story to another Bible story, how could they relate them to their own lives?

In the groundbreaking book *Already Gone*, authors Ken Ham, Britt Beemer, and Todd Hillard present some challenging data about our churches' education programs. They surveyed one thousand Americans between twenty and thirty years of age. The results showed that 95 percent of those interviewed attended church regularly during their elementary and middle school years, 55 percent during high school, down to a low of 11 percent during their college years. Almost 40 percent of the respondents began having doubts about the authority of the Scriptures in middle school—sixth through eighth grades.

You might be thinking, "Thank goodness for our Sunday Schools!" What could be more important than giving middle schoolers a good grounding in the Scriptures just when they are starting to doubt things the most! But what the survey revealed may shock you as much as it did me. Kids who regularly attended Sunday School were significantly more likely to doubt the authority of Scripture! Consider, for example, these results:

	Attended Sunday School	Did not attend Sunday School
Believe that God used evolution to create human beings?	25.6%	18.5%
Believe that premarital sex is wrong?	47.7%	40.8%
Feel good people don't need to go to church?	39.3%	28.9%
Feel the church is relevant to your needs today?	46.4%	39.6%

The survey seems to indicate that Sunday School has not, generally, been the solution; it's been the problem. Stunned? I was. Some Sunday School graduates see the Bible as just a bunch of stories, no different from fiction and certainly not believable in our modern, scientific age. (This is not to say that Sunday School is a bad discipline; however, as we'll discuss shortly, how we teach it needs to be rethought.)

What, then, is the solution? A wholesale rethinking of how we teach the Scriptures, realizing that we are teaching the Bible to children growing up in a scientific mental environment. We need to teach the Scriptures as history and not simply a bunch of disconnected stories. We also need to address those things in Scripture that fly in the face of our scientific, materialistic, and atheistic environment. We need to challenge our children to think about biblical accounts in the safe environment of church, because they will certainly be challenged to think about them when they interact with the world.

We can think of our teaching as a vaccination against the disease of the devil's lies. When we vaccinate, we inject a small amount of a real disease into the body so the immune system is prepared when the real thing comes along. We should not be afraid to expose kids to secular world thinking. If we don't do it in small doses, in a safe environment, our children will face the full onslaught of the disease with

Let your kids know that no question is off limits. Be known as a person to whom they can ask anything and even express their doubts.

no built-up resistance. Otherwise, our children may assume we ignored the questions because we had no good answers.

You may know of Professor Bart Ehrman, who has been on many popular television and radio shows. Dr. Ehrman was raised in a very conservative Christian home and attended a fairly conservative Christian church. By the time he completed his graduate work in New Testament studies, however, he had lost his belief in the full authority of the New Testament as the actual, inspired, and inerrant Word of God. In graduate school, he was confronted for the first time with the actual data of the New Testament manuscripts, and the concept of textual criticism made it difficult for him to accept that the Bible has divine origin. Ehrman is a great example of what can happen when we, with good intentions, shelter children from information we think will harm their faith. A better approach is to be honest about what we know and to show how that data is compatible with our beliefs. Then, when our children grow up and encounter people who interpret the data differently, they will be better prepared to give a defense for their Christian faith.

How to Answer Kids' Questions in a Way That Builds Faith in Christ

What can parents, pastors, teachers, and other influential adults do to help children grow in their love and trust of the Scriptures in a scientific mental environment? Here are some practical things individuals can do to help.

1. Know what the big issues are, when they arise, and how.
I was sitting in my office one day when one of our preschool teachers came in with a concern. She had been letting her students watch the PBS show *Dinosaur Train* when she heard one of the characters on the show say that dinosaurs existed "millions of years ago." She knew that our congregation did not accept as a fact that the earth is billions of years old or that dinosaurs existed millions of years before humans.

Thank the Lord for faithful teachers like her! She could easily have shrugged off what she heard, assuming it wouldn't impact the kids. She could have been embarrassed and decided not to mention it. Instead, she recognized an opportunity to address a significant issue where secular science clashes with the history given to us by our Lord. She embraced the challenge and sought help.

In a world where even TV shows geared toward preschoolers conflict with the Scriptures, is it any wonder that our middle schoolers question their faith? There is simply no age too young at which to start clarifying some of these issues. When I was young, *The Flintstones* was on TV. Two families with two parents and their children, coexisting with dinosaurs. That show was a paragon of Christian values compared to what children are exposed to today.

Watch what your children watch, read what they read, and point out where it conflicts with Scripture and why. Learn the unbiblical and often unscientific assumptions behind some of the things presented as "fact."

The Scriptures teach that all sea, air, and land creatures were made, according to their kinds, on the fifth and sixth days of creation. That would include dinosaurs. So what happened to them? Creation scientists have well-developed theories on how the global catastrophe of Noah's day would have fossilized many creatures on earth. Their theories are consistent with much of what we observe of their remains today. Groups such as Answers in Genesis provide some great resources for kids that connect their love for dinosaurs with scientific and scriptural explanations for their origin and their extinction. Creation scientists also have some great resources dealing with the age of the earth and of the universe.

2. Introduce kids to the miraculous in science. It is unfortunate that secular children's media promote ideas that clash with Scripture. What is more unfortunate, in my opinion, is that they tend to ignore the science that supports faith in a creator God. This is an area where we need to teach kids some basic science that they may not learn otherwise.

A few years ago, I gave a presentation on science and the Bible at a youth gathering. Rather than spending an hour refuting scientific theories that clash with the Scriptures, I focused instead on theories that point to God. I looked at four basic scientific ideas based on observable data:

a) *Quantum mechanics:* At the turn of the twentieth century, most people thought we had a firm grasp on the nature of matter and energy. Everyone knew that gases, liquids, and solids were made up of small building blocks called electrons, neutrons, and photons. Energy could be described by fields. Light was a kind of energy made up of waves. Then came the discovery that light was made up of photons that could act either like a wave or like a particle, depending on whether someone was observing it. This rocked the world of physics. The theory of quantum mechanics led many physicists, such as Max Planck and Werner Heisenberg, to a strengthened religious faith. It meant that the world was not a clock wound up at the beginning of time and left to run, but something much more mysterious. Quantum mechanics suggests that many things we think of as impossible—like a man walking on water—may simply be highly improbable. Which means they could, theoretically and scientifically, happen.

b) *General relativity:* Another development in the early twentieth century that changed the way we look at the universe was the theory of general relativity. Einstein suggested that time, space, mass, energy, and length are related by the speed of light, which is constant in a vacuum regardless of the frame of reference. That means that at speeds approaching the speed of light, the size and mass of an object increases and time for that object slows down. It is difficult to exaggerate how much this theory changed the way we look at the universe. The idea that the world agreed with our intuition was irrevocably shaken. Religion was no longer the only field that asked people to believe something that seemed to go against common sense.

c) *Information theory:* To explain the wonder of DNA, I often compare our cells to a computer. The chemicals and structure of a DNA molecule are like a hard drive that stores genetic information. The four-letter DNA code that stores the genetic information is like the operating system that runs a computer. Neo-Darwinian evolution requires not only that the hard drive, the DNA structure, evolve through natural means but also that the operating system to make the information useful evolve at the same time. Even Francis Crick, co-discoverer of the shape of DNA, thought it highly unlikely that it occurred through some natural evolutionary process. A committed atheist, Crick chose to believe that some alien race created or brought life to earth.

d) *Habitable zones:* Nicolaus Copernicus was one of the first scientists to propose that the earth and all the planets revolve around the sun. Later, astronomers discovered that our sun is not at the center of the galaxy, but rather far out in one spiral arm. Neither is our galaxy at the center of the universe. All these discoveries led some to use the phrase "Copernican Principle" to suggest that earth and its inhabitants are nothing special. But Christian astronomer Guillermo Gonzalez turned that idea on its ear when he published a paper on what he called "galactic habitable zones." In the book *The Privileged Planet*, which he co-authored with Jay Richards, Gonzalez suggested that the earth is actually in a sweet spot not only for life, but for the possibility of studying and appreciating the universe as a whole. Earth, it turns

Learn some good, basic science that supports belief in God, and show how the Scriptures point in the direction of that science.

out, is special in numerous ways, including where we are located in our solar system and in our galaxy. The odds of finding a planet just like earth are astonishingly small.

3. Build up a kids' library. Just as every congregation should have a collection of books and other resources addressing adult questions about science and faith, we should also have resources available for kids. With a little research and pastoral guidance, you can assemble a range of affordable, engaging books that discuss creation, the flood, dinosaurs, evolution, genetics, and more.

How Congregations Can Strengthen Our Children's Faith in the Word of God

Some of what we've discussed can be done by individuals, families, small groups, or school associations. But what can congregations do to help children appreciate science and retain their love and trust in God's Word?

1. *Sunday School:* As the research presented earlier points out, Sunday School can be part of the problem. To make Sunday School work for us rather than against us requires some rethinking of the way we present accounts from the Bible.

First, emphasize the historical nature of the Bible's accounts. Use a history timeline, especially of the Old Testament, to place events in context. Use maps that include not only the old names of places (Babylon, Canaan, Jebus) but also their modern names (Iraq, Palestine/Israel, Jerusalem). Compare and contrast the distinctions between a fairy tale and a biblical account. When I teach the account of the great flood, for example, I often retell a popular fairy tale this way:

On the third day of the month, early in the morning, a girl by the name of Jenna who often wore a red riding hood left her home to make the six-mile trip to her grandmother's house. After two miles, she encountered a wolf, who proceeded to have a conversation with her about her destination and the purpose of her travels. After the one-hour conversation ended, Jenna Red Riding Hood proceeded on the exact same trail for an additional three miles . . .

Of course no one tells a fairy tale with those kinds of details. They're irrelevant to the story, which is the moral. Yet a reading of Genesis 6–9 will reveal an account filled with dates and measurements that are quite out of place in a fairy tale.

Second, when parents come across events in Scripture that seem to go against what is currently observed in nature or against secular scientific theories, they should talk about them with their children. If you have a question or a doubt about a particular event, children probably do too. Find out what scientists who accept the authority of Scripture say about these events. If there is no obvious answer, admit it. Point out, however, that there are other events recorded in Scripture that seem impossible, such as Jesus' resurrection, that are confirmed by multiple eyewitnesses.

In our congregation the Sunday School teachers and I study the upcoming lessons and address historical, geographical, and scientific issues that may arise. In this way teachers are prepared to address these concerns at age-appropriate levels.

2. *Vacation Bible School:* Many children who attend VBS are not exposed to the Bible at any other time. To be sure, we cannot teach and defend the entire council of God in the Scriptures in one week, but this is a wonderful, God-given opportunity to address some of these issues. We should take the same approach with VBS that we take with Sunday School; that includes putting events from the Scriptures in historical and geographical context and preparing teachers to address anything that might be troubling in our modern mental environment.

3. *Meet a Faithful Scientist Day:* We are blessed in our congregation to have two actual NASA rocket scientists, several doctors (including one who is an adjunct professor of pediatrics), and many geophysicists, geologists, and engineers. How exciting is it for kids to meet real, live scientists and engineers and discover that they are also Christians committed to the authority of Scripture? How great is it for them to hear a medical doctor explain that evolution plays no role in her day-to-day work? How uplifting is it to meet someone working to get men and women into space who believes that the Lord created the universe and all life on earth?

If there are no scientists in your congregation, ask neighboring congregations if they have qualified members who are interested in speaking. You could also contact your denominational headquarters, a creation science ministry, or a seminary. It's worth the money and time to build up the young children in your midst for whom Christ died.

Final Thoughts

The congregation's youth and children's ministries are essential to the church's life. Parents should also not underestimate their role in their child's education. Sunday School and confirmation classes are meant to supplement the role of the parent in faith education, not substitute for it. Be aware of what is taught in the public schools many of our kids attend. Ask teens how many times they heard the words "millions of years ago" in school this week. Help them deal with the contradictions between what they hear in school and what they hear in worship and Sunday School.

Key Points

- God calls us to teach our children His Word.

- It is not enough to simply teach children "Bible stories." We should teach the true biblical history of the world (which the world does its best to contradict).

- Don't hesitate to teach children the miraculous in science. Most of what we can observe in the world supports, rather than contradicts, God's Word.

Introduce kids to the wonders of God's creation from a biblical perspective.

- Evaluate Sunday School and Vacation Bible School curricula, as well as children's libraries, to ensure that they meet the needs of children who will grow up in a scientific mental environment.

Discussion Questions

1. Have you been a part of your congregation's children's ministry? Why or why not? How might you get involved in this important ministry?

2. What children's movies or television shows are you familiar with? Do they support or contradict the history of the world as taught by Scripture? How can you help children deal with what they hear outside of the church setting?

Action Items

1. Do you interact regularly with kids? If so, resolve to listen to the questions they ask, and be someone to whom they might address their questions. Help them deal with their questions in a responsible way.

2. If you are involved in a congregation's children's or youth ministry, evaluate your Sunday School, VBS, and confirmation curricula. Do they address kids who live in a scientific mental environment?

If not, find new curricula or introduce changes to the ones you are using. Encourage teachers to be aware of the issues. Give them materials that can address kids' questions.

I am a visual learner and a hands-on learner

too. When it comes to the teachings of the Scriptures and the Lutheran Confessions, I have always learned and taught them best by visualizing them and showing how they work out in everyday life. Take the doctrine of God's tri-unity, that God is three in person yet one in essence. If God is simply one "being" like us, then He remains outside us, distant from our cares and concerns. If He exists only within us, our worship could easily become self-idolatry. But God is the Father who watches over us and all creation, the Son who relates to us even in our fallen state, and the Holy Spirit who works God's will within us. Our theology, drawn from the Scriptures and summarized in our creeds and Confessions, helps us picture a God who is over us, with us, and in us, yet remains one God. The doctrines of the Scriptures are pictures that help us to rightly know and worship the God who seeks us out to save us.

The Scriptures are also filled with visual imagery of another kind, pictures of the kind of people God intended us to be. If we ask the average American what Christianity is all about, he or she would probably answer "to be a better person." My wife, who teaches at a Lutheran elementary school, asked the kids in her class early in the school year what makes us right with God. Most of her students answered "being good." If we ask what it means to be "good," many people would probably point to the Ten Commandments.

Don't murder, don't steal, and don't cheat on your husband or wife. They would point to a list of rules.

Yes, God's Ten Commandments in the Bible paint a picture of how being good looks. So does the New Testament, where our Lord (and then His apostles) used stories, illustrations, and often long strings of adjectives to give us a picture of what a "good" person should look like. Consider the parable of the Good Samaritan. When Jesus was asked "who is my neighbor?" He didn't give a definition. He told a story to illustrate what a neighbor would look like in action (Luke 10:25–37). When Jesus was asked who would be the greatest in the kingdom of God, He didn't list the qualifications that person needed. He showed what He expected by how He responded to a child (Mark 9:33–37). Jesus did more than talk about the Law. He lived out the Law and became the only example in history of what a human would look like if we were as God intended us to be in the beginning.

Paul took a somewhat different tact in his Epistles, but one that I think served the same purpose. He grabbed a bunch of adjectives and threw them together to paint a picture of a human being. We do a real injustice to these passages when we try to tease them apart and make them into a sermon series or prolonged Bible study. These words are meant to be read frequently and as a whole, that the Spirit might use them to shape God's baptized children. Consider, for example, Colossians 3:12–16:

Put on then, as God's chosen ones, holy and beloved, compassionate hearts, kindness, humility, meekness, and patience, bearing with one another and, if one has a complaint against another, forgiving each other; as the Lord has forgiven you, so you also must forgive. And above all these put on love, which binds everything together in perfect harmony. And let the peace of Christ rule in your hearts, to which indeed you were called in one body. And be thankful. Let the word of Christ dwell in you richly, teaching and admonishing one another in all wisdom, singing psalms and hymns and spiritual songs, with thankfulness in your hearts to God.

Paul knew that for Christians the Law was no longer a thing that comes from the outside but is now embedded in us by the Holy Spirit. Paul expected that these words would take root in our hearts and shape our lives. God would change us through them and conform us to the image of Jesus (Romans 8:29). Paul understood visual learners, which is why he urged his listeners not to "do the Law" (abstract) but to "be imitators of me" (concrete) (1 Corinthians 4:16; 11:1; 2 Thessalonians 3:9).

This chapter is about Scripture, science, and ethics. It is about living as Christians in a world where science often has an impact before we've had a chance to evaluate the consequences. It is about the need to model what it looks like to be human to a world that no longer understands what that means. Christian ethics is not about the wagging of fingers at others or about judging those who have it wrong. It is about showing a still more excellent way by what we say and how we act.

How Science and Scripture Ethically Collide

When Martin Luther wrote his Small Catechism, he lived in a generation where theft meant fixing the scales at your store, adultery meant cheating on your spouse, and murder meant stabbing someone to death. When we entered the twentieth century, new questions arose that Luther could not have considered, and The Lutheran Church—Missouri Synod responded by producing additional questions and answers to Luther's original work, resulting in a Small Catechism "with Explanation." Now, science is progressing at such speed that even this expanded book has a hard time keeping up. The basic tools are still there but must now be applied to situations such as these:

- A woman has the genome of the unborn child in her womb sequenced. She learns that her child has a high risk for physical deformities. Should she abort the child, who may be a financial drain on her already tight family budget and who may spend his life suffering from illness and the stigma attached to it?

- Some scientists believe they have identified the physical cause for same-sex gender attraction. Since being gay or lesbian can no longer be considered a choice but rather a natural inclination, should Christians reconsider how they interpret the Scriptures on the matter of marriage and family?

- A family loses a beloved four-year-old in a car accident. Scientists offer to take the child's DNA and produce a cloned embryo, which the mother could then carry to term. How would a Christian friend respond?

- An 86-year-old grandfather is diagnosed with a form of cancer that has a 60-percent survival rate. Because of restrictions on his insurance coverage, the treatment will cost more than $150,000. Should the treatment be successful, doctors believe his life will be extended by five to ten years. The grandfather does not want to burden his family and wants to know if declining treatment would be considered euthanasia.

- A young woman is struggling to pay her college tuition and has been offered ten thousand dollars for some of her eggs by a fertility clinic. Should she sell her eggs to help finance her future?

Some of these are real-life examples of questions I've heard or have been asked; some are situations that are just around the corner. Christians often think of science and Scripture colliding on questions of the universe's origin or the possibility of miracles, but the two increasingly intersect in the arena of ethics.

Look for ethical questions in news stories with a scientific angle, and ask what basic scriptural insights apply.

Duns Scotus was a Christian philosopher and theologian in the Middle Ages. He is best known for inventing an ingenious method of argumentation. When defending a Christian doctrine, he would first ask, "Could God have done it?" If the answer was yes, he would ask, "Would it be a fitting thing for God to do?" If that answer was yes, he would conclude that God therefore must have done it. Many people use the same form of argumentation when it comes to ethics and science. "Can we do it?" Science answers yes. "Would it be fitting for us, as a scientific people, to do it?" If yes, then of course we should do it. But this second question is sometimes not even asked. In 1949, Elvin Stakman, then president of the American Association for the Advancement of Science, quipped that "science cannot stop while ethics catches up." It's not so much that science can't stop as it is that science won't.

Yet many scientists welcome a Christian voice on these issues. While some welcome the idea that technology will replace spirituality and religion, others, such as scientist Jaron Lanier, quoted in Joel Garreau's book *Radical Evolution*, wish religion would step out of the shadows and speak out on how changes in medicine affect our humanity.

Christians are well-known for drawing the line on ethical questions. We are known for saying "thus far and no further." We understand that life is sacred, a gift from God. We know that life begins at conception and that our lives are known by God even before that (Jeremiah 1:5). Life is not ours to give, and it is not ours to take without God's leave. We also know that this life is only a passing shadow, a dress rehearsal for a new age that is yet to come. Death is the wages of sin, but in Christ death is not the end. Though life is sacred, we do not hold on to it at all costs: "Yes, we are of good courage, and we would rather be away from the body and at home with the Lord. So whether we are at home or away, we make it our aim to please Him" (2 Corinthians 5:8–9).

How do we apply these principles to specific ethical problems, recognizing that our calling as Christians is to model what it means to be human in the midst of a fallen world? Have we demonstrated to the world how our faith helps us think about organ transplants, gene therapy, and advance health care directives (such as living wills)? Are the scientists and engineers in our congregations, especially those working in areas they find ethically challenging, lifted up in prayer? Do we give positive direction and modeling or only legalistic guidelines on these issues? Do we, in all things, proclaim the Gospel of Jesus Christ, who died for our failures that we might have life in His name?

Issues on the Immediate Horizon

The questions I asked at the opening of the previous section point to some of the immediate ethical challenges on the horizon. Here are some I think every congregation should discuss, with a view toward how to model Christian ethics as individuals and as a community.

1. *Infertility:* One out of every ten couples is unable to conceive a child naturally. My wife and I are one of those couples, so I speak from experience. One of the first commandments given to man and woman after creation was to go forth and multiply, and most couples desire to fulfill that command. We still want families, despite the costs and the secular doom-and-gloom view of the future. In times past, the options for barren couples were limited: childlessness or adoption. Today, however, the options are limited only by your pocketbook and your ethics.

At the end of a series of medical tests, my wife and I sat before our doctor and received the news: first, we would likely never conceive without medical intervention; and second, such intervention was possible. One intervention offered us was in vitro fertilization. In and of itself, this does not raise huge ethical issues. The child is still the product of a husband and wife. The problem is that many children are created in vitro, but few are chosen to survive. Multiple fertilized eggs are implanted in the mother's womb. Some, perhaps four or five, will successfully implant. At a certain stage of growth, all but one or two of these children will be killed, resulting in (it is hoped) at least one child that is born. Many Christians who choose this treatment will not allow any of the babies to be killed, resulting in the live births of five, six, or seven children. But is this a God-pleasing way to address barrenness?

My wife and I could not consider this a God-pleasing option. Our doctor, however, insisted that many "religious people" use in vitro fertilization. A local Islamic imam, he told us, declared that a fetus is only a child after twenty-two weeks of gestation—coincidentally, the exact time at which babies are terminated in the mother's womb during the fertility treatment.

For us, adoption was the better model of human—Christian—behavior. There are millions of children already in the world who do not have parents, something that God did not intend for them. And we now have two wonderful daughters who are our children in a similar way to how we are the Father's children: by adoption (Galatians 4:4–5).

How do we model Christian care and concern for the barren couples around us? Do we joke with them about "when they're going to start a family," not realizing the pain they feel? Do we feel bad for adoptive parents because they don't have "children of their own"? How can we show that sometimes science does not provide a better solution than God's Word, which speaks so highly of adoption?

Christians are adopted, not born, into God's family. What a beautiful picture of God's love in Christ when Christians adopt children into their earthly families! Counselors at Christian agencies would be happy to discuss the process with you. Take a step of faith and think about welcoming a child into your home through adoption.

2. *Use of Technology:* Canadian philosopher Marshall McLuhan coined many phrases that are now a part of our vocabulary. "Global village" is one. His most famous statement, however, is that "the medium is the message." McLuhan meant that the method used to communicate ideas shape us as much as the ideas themselves.

Since Johannes Gutenberg invented moveable type and revolutionized printing, the media through which most of our information has come have been the written page and the spoken word. If you wanted to absorb new ideas, you sat down with a book presenting those ideas or in front of a teacher lecturing about them. The next technology to profoundly change teaching and learning was the television. Visuals, such as the woodcuts of Luther's time or the stained glass windows and statuary of European cathedrals, had been used to communicate information for centuries. But these had a permanency which television does not. Television allows images to change as rapidly as words can be spoken. It was the introduction of television into culture that gave rise to McLuhan's insight about the relationship between medium and message.

Western society has moved past the age of the television. We now live in the age of the Internet: hyperlink, smartphone, text message, and social media. The work environment of many Americans forces the kind of multitasking that severely limits attention span. Our children's environment is not much better. Neuroscientists are concerned that our brains are losing the ability to focus.

What do we, as Christians and as Christian churches, have to say about this change to our brains? We are not just people of books but people of *the* book, the Bible. Do we ask whether technology is making us more or less human? Do we ask ourselves how we can be in the world and still show that we are not of it? The world needs us to model the

Be wise about the technology you use. Think about how you use it and what effect it may have on you and those around you.

Christian worldview, even if it doesn't know that. We are the priests for the world, and being salt and light in the world is an important part of our calling as God's children in Christ Jesus (1 Peter 2:9–10; Matthew 5:13–15).

3. *Genetic Information:* A few years ago, a member of my wife's family was tested for a genetic marker that would predispose him to blood clots. His doctor suggested everyone in the family take the test, so they could know whether to take preventative health measures. Thinking that it would be better to plan ahead than to be surprised by an aneurism, my wife took the test. Since then, she has been ineligible for private health insurance because of this "preexisting condition." Knowledge, even knowledge that can help us stay healthy, has consequences.

A decade ago the cost of sequencing one human's genome was close to a hundred million dollars. Now it can be done for less than ten thousand. Companies such as Life Technologies Corporation say that soon they will reduce that to around the cost of the average MRI scan. But that knowledge will come with consequences. How will health insurance work in a world where almost everyone will have a "preexisting condition"? How will we distinguish between the genetic predisposition for acquiring a disease and having the disease itself? What about testing children before birth? Are we prepared to defend our understanding of the preciousness of life even when we know a child will be born with a debilitating disease?

The temptation for the Church is to shout our answers at the world, to create hard and fast ethical rules and condemn loudly those who violate them. I urge us to pursue another path, that of a community that models Christian—human—behavior. We must study the Scriptures and our Lutheran Confessions for the principles needed to guide our use of genetic information. We should be discussing these issues and learning to model appropriate responses.

4. *Care and Its Cost:* Everyone is aware of the rising cost of health care. What few realize is that much of the increase is due to ongoing scientific advancement, especially in pharmaceuticals. Diseases and conditions that could not be treated half a century ago can now be addressed—for a price. Consider a cancer drug that could extend the patient's life by up to four months, but at cost of $100,000.

When your doctor brings up questions that have to do with genetics, ask how it might affect your current insurance coverage or your eligibility to be insured in the future.

Not everyone has access to these types of drugs, of course. The world average personal income in 2007 was

$7,000. That figure is an average, so it includes the annual incomes of people like Bill Gates and Warren Buffett. The average income of a worker in India was $1,000 a year. The cost of such drug treatment is simply out of reach of most people.

Think about what it means to be healthy as a Christian and how that impacts your health-care decisions.

It seems likely, given the current state of medical science, that new treatments will continue to be developed for a multitude of diseases at ever-increasing costs. It is now possible to bankrupt one's self to pursue a short extension on life. How does our Lord want us to approach these issues? Do Christian ethics demand that we extend our earthly lives at any price? Are we required to help extend the lives of all people at all costs? Medical science is not waiting for our answer. But at some point, someone close to us will be faced with a complex medical decision. How will we help them with the decision? How will we support them once the decision is made, especially if it's not what we would have chosen?

Scanning the Distant Horizon

Christians should not be content to simply wait for the world to make poor decisions and then react as armchair quarterbacks. We should be proactive and prophetic, taking to heart Paul's words to the Ephesians:

> For at one time you were darkness, but now you are light in the Lord. Walk as children of light (for the fruit

of light is found in all that is good and right and true),
and try to discern what is pleasing to the Lord.
Take no part in the unfruitful works of darkness,
but instead expose them. . . . Look carefully then
how you walk, not as unwise but as wise, making
the best use of the time, because the days are evil.
Therefore do not be foolish, but understand what
the will of the Lord is. (5:8–11, 15–17)

I've been an avid reader of science fiction since I was young. Most fans of science are! Science fiction fans often distinguish between "soft" fiction, which is set in the future or out in space, and "hard," which explores the boundaries of current scientific theory and tries to remain faithful to what we know now is possible. Good hard science fiction has predicted or prefigured many things we now take for granted. Satellites and global positions systems, the Internet, PDAs, cell phones, and prosthetic limbs were all once fiction and are now reality. Hard science fiction can open our minds to things that science is currently exploring and give us a chance to think about them in light of Christ and the Scriptures before they happen.

One subject often dealt with in hard science fiction is longevity or anti-aging treatments. Some contemporary scientists such as Ray Kurzweil devote a lot of time and resources to cheating physical death through advanced medicine. Is it possible to stop the aging process? Not yet, but if it becomes possible, how should Christians respond? Do we truly place our hope for the future in "the life of the world to come," as the Nicene Creed says? Would forgoing anti-aging treatment be a form of euthanasia and transgress the Fifth Commandment?

> Imagine what a Christian congregation might look and act like in the twenty-second century.

I despair that, with few exceptions, religion finds only a small place in the future described by most science fiction authors. This seems to me to indicate a real chasm between the world of science and the world of the Scriptures. Writer and theologian Marva Dawn has accused Christians of lacking the sanctified imagination that Christians in the past have shown. Why should those whom the Holy Spirit indwells not be able to "see" a world with Christ, rather than leave atheists to imagine a world without him? Who better to help sinful, fallen humanity come to grips with our need to repent in the face of tragedy than Christians? Who better to help humanity see where sin might lead us than those who understand what sin is, where it came from, and who can deliver us from it?

Final Thoughts

Christians need to model human behavior in our world. As scientific advances change the way we live and how we think, it is more important than ever for Christians and Christian congregations to live in Christ for the sake of the world. Consider these words from the anonymous Epistle to Diognetus, written sometime in the second century AD:

Christians are distinguished from other men neither by country, nor language, nor the customs which they observe. . . . But, inhabiting Greek as well as barbarian cities, according as the lot of each of them has determined, and following the customs of the natives in respect to clothing, food, and the rest of their ordinary conduct, they display to us their wonderful and confessedly striking method of life. They dwell in their own countries, but simply as sojourners. As citizens, they share in all things with others, and yet endure all things as if foreigners. Every foreign land is to them as their native country, and every land of their birth as a land of strangers. They marry, as do all [others]; they beget children; but they do not destroy their offspring. They have a common table, but not a common bed. They are in the flesh, but they do not live after the flesh. They pass their days on earth, but they are citizens of heaven. They obey the prescribed laws, and at the same time surpass the laws by their lives. (*The Ante-Nicene Fathers*, vol. 1, translated and edited by Alexander Roberts and James Donaldson, 1885)

Take time to think about what it means for you to live as a baptized child of God, redeemed from sin by Christ to live in Christ, even in this present age. Encourage your congregation to think about Christian ethics and how to address the issues we currently face and anticipate questions on the horizon.

Most important, strive to model for the world who you are: a newly created human in Jesus, God's only Son.

Key Points

- Christians and Christian congregations are called to model Christian behavior, individually and corporately.

- Science and the Scriptures collide not just on the questions of origins or miracles, but also on the issue of ethics.

- Advancements in science outpace our ability to evaluate their value, but science will not wait for Christians to give research the green or red light.

- Christians are called by God to evaluate how we can best use technology, rather than allowing ourselves to be used by it.

Discussion Questions

1. Have you or someone you know made an ethical decision brought on by advances in science or technology? How did you arrive at a decision? Did your Christian faith influence that decision? Why or why not?

Action Items

1. Start a discussion group to explore issues arising on the frontiers of science. Read science fiction together and explore the implications of the books.

2. Ask your pastor or a knowledgeable layperson to lead a study on health-care issues in light of the Scriptures.

Over the last two centuries, we have learned innumerable things about how the universe and our planet work. We have made tremendous advances in climatology, biology, ecology, oceanography, and all sorts of sciences dealing with the earth and how it functions day-to-day, year-to-year, and century-to-century. In the first chapter, we discussed how preconceptions impact the interpretation of data, and in the third how our preconceptions about morality impact how we use scientific advances and technology. In this chapter, we'll consider how our understanding of the planet, both through science and the Scriptures, impacts our day-to-day lives in positive ways. We'll also talk about the impact of Christian stewardship on the way the culture views our congregations and the Gospel.

We live in a mental environment that sees our world as a speck of dust in a universe so vast that it boggles the mind. It takes four seconds for a beam of light to make the round-trip from the earth to its moon. The light from the sun reaches the earth after a full eight minutes, Jupiter after forty-three minutes, and Neptune after more than four hours. We are four and a half years traveling at the speed of light to the nearest star, more than 20,000 years traveling at light speed to the center of our galaxy, and 180,000 light years to our closest fully independent galactic neighbor, the Large Magellanic Cloud. But long before we could appreciate the size of the cosmos, David wrote:

O Lord, our Lord,
> how majestic is Your name in all the earth!
> You have set Your glory above the heavens. . . .

When I look at Your heavens, the work of Your fingers,
> the moon and the stars, which You have set in place,
> what is man that You are mindful of him,
and the son of man that You care for him?
(Psalm 8:1, 3–4)

Ask the average Christian what the relationship is between humans and creation, and he or she may respond that the world was created for our enjoyment and use. After all, the Lord told the first man and woman that they were to have dominion over all animals (Genesis 1:26). They were to "be fruitful and multiply and fill the earth and subdue it" (1:28). They were given all plants yielding seed and all trees bearing fruit for food (1:29).

Yet a proper understanding of these verses hinges entirely on what it means to have "dominion" and what it means to "subdue." We are fallen human beings, and when someone offers something that sounds like power, we tend to grab it with both hands! John Dalberg-Acton, a nineteenth-century British baron, famously said that "power tends to corrupt, and absolute power corrupts absolutely." Christians might modify that proverb, based on what we read in the Bible. We might say that "the corrupt use power corruptly, and absolute power in the hands of the corrupt will be used absolutely corruptly." Wordy, but true, given everything we know about our sinful nature. So when we come across words like "dominion" and "subdue"—instructions given before the fall—we fill them with post-fall meaning and intent.

Scripture paints a different picture of the purpose of creation: that the universe was not created for the pleasure of humanity but to reflect the glory of God. David puts it this way: "The earth is the LORD's and the fullness thereof, the world and those who dwell therein" (Psalm 24:1). Elsewhere David announces that "the heavens declare the glory of God, and the sky above proclaims His handiwork" (Psalm 19:1). In his Letter to the Romans, Paul points out that the creation is sufficient to give any clearheaded human, whose mind is not clouded by sin, knowledge of God's "invisible attributes, namely, His eternal power and divine nature" (1:20).

So what is humanity's role in creation? Are we no different from a three-toed sloth, a palm tree, or ocean plankton? Yes, indeed we are! We are the crown of creation, destined to bear the image of God within the cosmos. Adam and Eve were the last born of creation, just as Jesus, Adam's descendent through the Virgin Mary, is the firstborn of the new creation (Romans 8:29; Colossians 1:18). Our first parents were given dominion over all things and asked to subdue creation. But those are words of stewardship, not lordship.

Take the word *dominion*. I grew up in Canada, which in its early years was called "The Dominion of Canada." The founders of the British colony chose the term *dominion* carefully.

They wanted to reflect that the British crown—and above the crown, God Himself—had final authority over this vast land surrounded by three seas and the rebellious colonies to the south. The governors and parliamentarians of Canada did not own this land to do with as they saw fit. They were to have dominion over it in the stead of its true Lord. Their dominion did not mean "domination." It meant "careful and thoughtful stewardship."

In Genesis 1:28, "subdue" translates the Hebrew word *kabash*. Our old Adam would love to see that word as a call to "boss creation around." We have the same problem when we read Ephesians 5:22 and its call for women to submit to their husbands or Paul's instruction that we submit to one another out of reverence for Christ (Ephesians 5:21). Only a Christian, as a new creation, led and influenced by the Spirit given to us in Baptism and through the Scriptures, can rightly understand these words. The Lutheran Church—Missouri Synod's publication *Together with All Creatures* (2010) suggests that to subdue "may refer to the setting of boundaries even as God did so during the first three days" (p. 40, expanded version). In light of the many passages that identify God as the owner of creation and His glory as its purpose, this understanding of "subdue" makes much more sense.

Read the LCMS Commission on Theology and Church Relations document *Together With All Creatures* and study it individually and as a congregation.

What does all this mean? Christians, who by the power

of the Spirit bear again the full image of God alongside their old Adam, are to model for the world how to have dominion over God's good but fallen creation and how to use it wisely as stewards, not tyrannical overlords.

How the World Sees Stewardship Differently

Those outside the Church and under the exclusive sway of their fallen nature treat the created world very differently. In fact there are two worldviews that guide non-Christians (and even some Christians) in their actions toward the created world. The first view is that the world is an object to be exploited. The second is that the world is an improbable, fragile accident that needs to be protected at all costs. Neither is the Christian worldview, and both lead to behaviors that Christians find appropriate and inappropriate.

As I explained earlier, people who see the world as an object to be exploited come to that view based on presuppositions. A presupposition that the universe came about through a cosmic accident and that all life is here by chance could inspire that worldview. Paul mentions this kind of view in First Corinthians. He suggests that if there is no God and no resurrection and restoration in Jesus Christ, then "Let us eat and drink, for tomorrow we die" (15:32). Why preserve the earth for future generations when it will cost my personal pleasure here and now? Others with this worldview may have come to it by misunderstanding Scripture. They think that God gave humans dominion over creation and called upon us to subdue it; therefore, whatever a human does to show creation who's boss must be pleasing in God's eyes.

Ironically the same idea—that we and the universe came from nothing and are going nowhere—has led many people in the opposite direction. They believe that because our planet and the life on it came about by accident, and an improbable accident at that, we'd better look after it carefully. Basically, we got lucky once; we are unlikely to get so lucky a second time. A subset of this particular group is responsible for a lot of the climate change scare. Climate change is a developing science, and there is evidence that the earth's climate is indeed changing. If you believe the earth and its ecosystems are here solely by chance, then you might also believe that humans could easily and permanently destroy it. You might even think you are justified in twisting the truth so as to save this very precious and unsupervised (at least by a god) commodity.

The Christian response to both these worldviews is that the earth, the life on it, and the entire universe in which it exists are not here by accident. There is a Creator, who made all things good in the beginning. Life is intentional, and the Lord intended for the world to exist without death. The corruption of creation that we see all around us, and that Paul writes about in Romans 8, is a consequence of sin. But the same God who created the universe continues to sustain it. The cosmos will remain under His providential care until the Last Day. In the meantime, we are to take up our original charge to be good stewards of the world, even in its fallen state.

How Christians Steward God's Creation

How do Christians model good stewardship? There are many practical ways that emphasize creation as a reflection of God's glory and humanity's distinct place as its stewards. We are part of the earth's biosphere, but in the same way that the president of the United States is also an American citizen. We are part of life on earth, a unique part with a special leadership task. Here are some suggestions:

1. *Pollution:* I suggest that for Christians a pollutant is anything that aggravates life on earth and detracts from God's glory in creation. Everything that changes the environment is not necessarily a pollutant; every change to the environment is not necessarily pollution. That is a significant difference between the Christian view of pollution and the non-Christian view. Flooding a large area to create a reservoir that will generate hydroelectric power may be seen by many as polluting the environment. Certainly reservoirs have changed the landscape significantly. But so did the great flood. So long as we work to minimize impact, we can create electricity without aggravating human life or detracting from the beauty of creation.

It is undeniable that humans pollute in ways that can aggravate life. Just as science and technology have created these problems, however, so can science and technology find solutions. Mass transit that uses electricity generated from wind farms, solar panels, nuclear energy, or clean coal can significantly reduce urban air pollution, as will the hybrid and electric cars of the future. As Christians, we ought to be aware of the ways in which we contribute to pollution and be on the lookout for new technologies that will improve things.

2. Reduce: We live in a disposable society. Nothing is built to last; many of the devices we depend on have a planned obsolescence. It is difficult to live in the world and not succumb to the temptation to pitch and replace on a regular basis. Sometimes it is necessary, but not always. As Christians, we live in the world, but we are not of the world. Let us be wise as serpents and innocent as doves when it comes to our devices. Don't let the world tell you what you need; let Jesus' teachings guide you to know the difference between a simple want and a necessity.

My wife and I own two vehicles, one ten years old and one sixteen, and I feel the temptation to upgrade. Yet there is nothing wrong with our cars, and so long as we keep them tuned up and in good shape, we are keeping two more piles of metal out of car graveyards a while longer. We're also saving two car payments, which has enabled us to increase our tithe.

Think about all the things you would like to replace that really don't need to be replaced. Be aware that the world seeks after many things, but we are to seek after the kingdom of God (Matthew 6:25–33). We are to seek after Christ who has redeemed us, not the things of a world that remains in bondage.

Think about the ways you generate pollution every day and what common sense things (conserving water and electricity, recycling) you can do to reduce the pollution you create.

3. *Reuse:* For the last thirty years, plastic bags have become the means of choice for bringing home groceries. My family brings home five to ten bags each time we shop for groceries. But what happens then? There are only so many uses for all those plastic bags. We keep a stash of reusable grocery bags in our cars to use instead of plastic grocery bags. The result is fewer plastic bags to throw out, recycle, or dispose of otherwise.

A couple of years ago, I attended a science and faith conference in Austin, Texas. After a session on science, Christianity, and the environment, several hundred of us headed to the lobbies outside the auditorium for a cup of coffee. Within minutes, dozens of disposable coffee cups were tossed into garbage cans. It looked to me that I was the only one who had brought a refillable mug. We do the same thing in many of our churches and workplaces. Why not buy a quality insulated mug and bring it with you? It keeps your coffee hot much longer than a disposable cup, which results (at least for me) in less wasted coffee. Think of the money the average congregation could save if they used refillable mugs.

4. *Don't Trash It:* As the old proverb goes, "one man's trash is another man's treasure." We often put something into the trash without a second thought for other ways to dispose of it. My family is blessed to live in a city with a great re-

Think about something you want to replace. Do you really need to, or do you simply want to? Think about what Christ would have you do with the money you might spend.

cycling program. We usually find that at the end of the week, our recycling bin has two to three times as much in it as our garbage bin. Between recycling, composting, reusing, selling, and donating, there isn't much left in the trash. Before you throw something out ask yourself three questions. Can I (1) sell it, (2) donate it, or (3) recycle it?

Selling unwanted items has never been easier. The technology of the Internet has enabled companies like eBay, Craigslist, and other swap-sites to do a booming business. If you have something worth selling but don't know how to use one of these sites, find someone who does. Have a garage or yard sale. Have your congregation or your neighborhood sponsor one.

Many groups take donations of gently used items. Some will even come to your house to pick up the items. Our local ministerium operates a thrift store, with profits supporting the services it provides. Many organizations accept old cars as donations, giving the owner a tax deduction based on the car's value.

Think about something you do every day or week that involves something disposable that could be replaced by something reusable.

If you can't sell it or donate it, then you can recycle it or compost it. We have a small composter in our backyard into which we place much of our kitchen waste. The final product often goes on our flower beds, saving us from having to buy potting soil. Most home renovation stores sell composters.

5. *Whole Life Stewardship:* You may have caught a pattern to the things we've been discussing. Good Christian stewardship of the environment is closely tied to good financial stewardship. God has given us everything we have. The earth is His, and by His grace we get to inhabit it, enjoy it, and care for it. Through it, God sustains us. Careful stewardship of resources is inextricably tied with careful management of the money with which God has gifted us. Secular environmentalists may make proposals that sound good but can be devastating to the economic life of people around the world. Being a good steward should not hurt our neighbor but help him to "improve and protect his possessions and income," and "help and support him in every physical need" (Small Catechism, Seventh and Fifth Commandments).

Beware of approaches to environmental stewardship that are Trojan horses for beliefs or values foreign to the Scriptures. Especially beware of people who try to manipulate science to support a particular interpretation of data.

6. *Service with Joy:* For many outside the Church, good stewardship of the resources and planet God has given us is a hardship or is done out of fear. "If we don't do the right thing, we will destroy the planet." "If we don't do something now, life as we know it will end." We have all heard doomsday predictions meant to motivate us to be better stewards. But such scenarios assume

Ask yourself if there is an alternative to throwing something in the trash. What options would be practical for your household?

no divine providence over the world, no God overseeing His creation. They assume that humanity is on its own in the universe. If there is no one in charge but us, if there is only science, which has done so much damage, what hope can there be for the future?

Christian stewardship of the environment flows from a belief that the universe and our world are not accidents but the results of purposeful, divine creative acts. We are not the chance products of millions of years of accidental chemical interactions but the specific creation of a loving God who called us to be caretakers of creation. True, we are fallen and our world has fallen with us. But God will continue to sustain the world until the day of our Lord Jesus Christ's return. As sons and daughters of God, we therefore serve within creation and over creation with joy. It's an exciting privilege to have our proper role restored by Jesus Christ!

How Being a Good Steward Is Being a Good Witness to Christ

There is one thing that all Christians and non-Christians share: our world. God has given us this one world and sustains us on it through His providence. He causes the rain to fall on the Christian and non-Christian alike (Matthew 5:45).

When others say we must do something for the sake of the environment, find out if anything else is motivating their views.

You don't need to be a son or daughter of God through Jesus Christ to realize the uniqueness of our planet.

It should not be a surprise, then, that non-Christians want to look after our world. The non-Christian worldview that science is all there is and that science proves we are a giant, cosmic accident has thrown non-Christians into something of a panic about the environment. Suppose we destroy this fragile world, which we inherited simply by luck? What if our luck turns?

Christians are often surprised at how vehemently non-Christians attack them as being anti-science. One example is Bill Nye, who has spoken strongly against adults who teach children that the universe is the creation of a loving God and that humans are here by design. In a 2012 editorial for the Montreal newspaper *La Presse*, one man argued that laws should be passed outlawing the teaching of religion to children until they reach the age of consent. Non-Christians feel that a Christian worldview will lead people to destroy the earth. If that happens, what will happen to life as we know it?

Christians can counter this argument by being what God called Adam and Eve to be: responsible stewards. What a wonderful witness if Christians are seen as respecting creation, not destroying it! Such stewardship can be a powerful witness in two ways. First, it demonstrates to non-Christians that we are not a threat to humanity's existence. They may continue to act as if we are, but as Peter writes, "Those who revile your good behavior in Christ may be put to shame" (1 Peter 3:16).

Do not labor in the world as those who have no hope, but as those who have been saved and restored by Jesus.

Second, it demonstrates what we profess in the First Article of the Nicene Creed (and the Apostles' Creed): our belief in "one God, the Father Almighty, maker of heaven and earth and of all things visible and invisible." We confess that the whole creation is the work of God, sustained by God, and reflects His glory. What better way to demonstrate our commitment in our hearts to those words of our lips than by respecting our Lord's creation?

Final Thoughts

In Matthew 28:18, Jesus told His disciples that "All authority in heaven and on earth has been given to Me." It is worth noting that there is a period at the end of this sentence. Jesus does not relinquish or delegate that authority; it remains His! He calls upon His disciples to make more disciples precisely because He is the one with authority over all things. His authority extends over all creation. Start a group in your church, formally or informally, to discuss how Christians can demonstrate our belief in a creator God through our stewardship of the earth and its resources. Think about what you can do as an individual. You are a child of God, and by God's Spirit, you can do it!

Key Points

- Creation was primarily created not for the benefit of humanity but to reflect God's glory.

- Adam and Eve were created to be the stewards, caretakers, of creation, not its overlords.

- Non-Christians often see the world either as an object to be abused and exploited or as a lucky accident that needs to be protected at all costs.

- Christians see the world as a sign of God's providence and power and, as His forgiven children, are excited to resume the caretaker role that Adam and Eve were given in the beginning.

- Stewardship of the earth and financial stewardship are tied together. Done as Christians, the one often positively impacts the other.

Discussion Questions

1. Does the word *environmentalism* have positive or negative connotations to you? Why?

2. What do you often hear non-Christian environmentalists say that contradicts the Scriptures?

3. Thinking back to early chapters of this book, are there specific ways that science is used as a tool to push a particular worldview?

4. What does your church do that can be considered good environmental stewardship?

Actions Items

1. Start a group of three or four who can come up with creative ways for your congregation to improve its stewardship of resources.

2. Plan and promote a sale of items that congregation members no longer want.

3. Help members find ways to donate gently used items to charity rather than throwing them away.

There are many reasons why increasing numbers of young Americans are walking away from the Church and from religious faith altogether. In his book *You Lost Me*, David Kinnaman, president of the Barna Group, suggests that the reasons for this are complicated. Many are "nomads," people who consider themselves Christian but don't see the value of being engaged with a congregation. A smaller number are "exiles," struggling to figure out what it means to be Christian in the twenty-first century, but finding that many churches are uninterested in their struggle. The smallest group is the "prodigals," those who left Christianity because it doesn't make sense.

It's tempting to look for the relationship between science and the Scriptures as relevant only to that last, small group of lost people. Reconciling our modern, scientific views of the world with biblical history seems less important than addressing the needs of the nomads and exiles. Yes, we might be tempted to think, it is sad that some have lost their faith because Christianity doesn't make sense to them, but wouldn't it be more productive to focus on the issues that are important to the other 90 percent of disaffected young adults?

I suggest another way to read this data, that underlying the apathy of the nomads and the struggles of the exiles is the same issue that affects the prodigals: reconciling the

DOUBTS, SCIENCE, AND SCRIPTURE

Christian worldview with the mental environment in which we live. The research presented in chapter 2 bears out this interpretation. Consider first the largest group of young adults who left their congregations, the nomads. Almost half of them believe worship attendance is optional according to Kinnaman. Yet we read in the Book of Hebrews: "And let us consider how to stir up one another to love and good works, not neglecting to meet together, as is the habit of some, but encouraging one another, and all the more as you see the Day drawing near" (10:24–25).

These young adults consider themselves Christians, yet they seem to have a more relaxed view of God's Word. Lack of faith in the authority of the Bible must play some role in their leaving the Church.

Consider the next largest group of young adults to leave the church, the exiles. More than a third of this group, according to Kinnaman, want to follow Jesus in a way that makes sense in the technological and scientific world in which they live. A little less than a third say they want to find a way to be Christian that doesn't include separating themselves from their culture. We certainly want to avoid reading too much into these statements, but I detect in them a struggle to reconcile a biblical worldview with the prevailing scientific one presented to them daily. (It is certainly not their only concern, but I believe it plays a role.)

It is not unusual for Christians to have doubts. Consider Thomas, the very symbol of doubt, who questioned Jesus' resurrection. Even Paul refused to believe Jesus was anything but a false messiah until he encountered Jesus on the road to Damascus. Peter wrote about those who scoffed at the early Christians, saying, "Where is the promise of His coming? For ever since the fathers fell asleep, all things are continuing as they were from the beginning of creation" (2 Peter 3:4). Many of the great Christian thinkers and leaders of the last two millennia had periods when they were afflicted by doubts. What is unique about our time is the grand non-Christian world narrative that competes with God's narrative in the Scriptures.

Consider one of the greatest worldview debates in the Old Testament, the one between the prophets of Baal and the Lord's prophet Elijah. Many of God's people had chosen to follow Baal, the ancient god of the Canaanites, and the rest of the Canaanite pantheon. Few were left to follow the Lord who had delivered the Hebrews out of slavery in Egypt. Elijah pleaded passionately with the people, saying "How long will you go limping between two different opinions? If the LORD is God, follow Him; but if Baal, then follow him" (1 Kings 18:21). Things were arranged for the prophets of Baal to call upon their God to burn a bull as an offering, and for Elijah to call upon the God of Israel to do the same. Four hundred fifty prophets of Baal danced around their dead bull, cutting themselves and screaming for a response. Nothing happened. Then Elijah dowsed his bull with water three times, called upon the Lord, and had his bull consumed by fire. It was clear whose worldview was, practically speaking, the one that made more sense. The prophets of Baal were defeated, and the Lord carried the day.

In our day, science has stepped in to replace the Canaanite religion. The prophets of technology quickly build a microwave gun to cook the bull. The followers of the Lord call out to God, and many times the bull lays unconsumed. To people in the Western world, it would seem that the Christians are the prophets of Baal and the scientist stands in for Elijah. Science has helped us eradicate diseases such as smallpox, put men on the moon, and build cleaner cities, faster computers, and better communications systems. "What," says the nonreligious person, "can faith do compared to all that?"

Let us not lose sight of this fact: this is the environment into which Christ has called His Church into existence. It is an environment in which doubt has an edge, where the Gospel is not an option among many religions, and where religion itself is held in derision. The Church must be ready to help those within and without its circle deal with the doubts raised in our science-based mental environment.

Dealing with Our Doubts

The Augsburg Confession of 1530 was the first formal statement of faith of the German reformers who contested the teachings of the Roman Church. Philip Melanchthon, the theologian behind the confession, knew that the fourth article dealing with our justification before God by faith in Christ would be controversial. What he and the other reformers may not have been prepared for was the controversy surrounding the second article, which deals with original sin.

Our churches teach that since the fall of Adam (Romans 5:12), all who are naturally born are born with sin (Psalm 51:5), that is, without the fear of God, without trust in God, and with the inclination to sin (AC II).

The chief sin of fallen humans is that we doubt God's existence. If you don't fear or honor something, if you don't trust in it, you function as if it does not exist. Luther wrote about this in his explanation of the Lord's Prayer's petition "lead us not into temptation": "We pray in this petition that God would guard and keep us so that the devil, the world, and our sinful nature may not deceive us or mislead us into false belief, despair, and other great shame and vice" (Small Catechism, Sixth Petition).

Ask the average American to list the worst sins, and I doubt that he or she would list false belief and despair, never mind put them first. Yet Satan's work has always been to corrupt knowledge of God, and our fallen nature has been only too happy to buy what the devil is selling. We are by nature doubters.

In so far as we are Christians, however, we are new creations in Jesus by the Holy Spirit (2 Corinthians 5:17). The veil that separated us from true knowledge of God is lifted. We can read the Scriptures as an open book. And we can also rightly see God's invisible attributes displayed in His creation (Romans 1:20), something that had previously been completely hidden.

Nevertheless, there is a constant battle within between our reborn selves and our old fallen nature. The way forward is not to deny this battle, but to acknowledge it for what it is. The way past our doubts is not to ignore them but to confront them and defeat them by the power of God's Word. Both Thomas and Paul were doubters before they became committed apostles. What created, restored, and strengthened their faith in Jesus was encountering Him as the one who died and was resurrected. We can encounter that same Lord in the Scriptures and the Sacraments. Here are some ways to deal with doubts when they surface:

1. Name your doubts and research them. What is it, specifically, that Satan and your fallen nature are using against your faith? Identify the specific doubts, write them down, and deal with them. Every doubt you will ever encounter has been or is being encountered by other Christians! We can be encouraged by what others have discovered.

When you have doubts, check your congregation's library to see what resources are available. In addition, there are two Web sites already mentioned in this book that I go to when secular scientific reports and studies raise doubts. One is answersingenesis.org; the other is evolutionnews.org. The wonderful thing about doubt is that it works both ways. The world will cause us to have doubts about our faith, but God's Word also raises doubts about the world's interpretation of things.

2. Go to your pastor. Your local librarian doesn't know everything. Neither does your pastor. The benefit of consulting others is not that they always know the answers but that they usually know where to find them. If you come across something that causes you to doubt some aspect of the faith, take it to your spiritual leader. Ask him if he has encountered this question before. If he hasn't, he may know of someone who has. He may even know of someone in your congregation who has expressed the same doubt and found satisfying and faith-strengthening answers. It might also be helpful to identify a member of the congregation who has a particular interest in and aptitude for the sciences and a commitment to the authority of Scripture. That person could serve as a resource for people who experience such doubts.

3. Read books and articles that challenge the world's thinking. There are a great many books out there that deal with living the Christian life and cultivating a Christian spirituality. The problem is that many of them avoid discussion of the world's thought processes and mental environment. Develop a habit of reading books that confront doubts raised by the world's thinking. Find out who the authors are that question, from a scientific perspective, understandings of our world that are underpinned by flawed assumptions. I find that my faith is strengthened when I read articles and books by

DOUBTS, SCIENCE, AND SCRIPTURE

scientists who, through their sanctified reason, see the Scriptures confirmed in their study of creation.

Many people avoid these books out of fear that reading them will introduce or increase doubt. If you haven't picked up on this yet, the world will raise doubts no matter how much you think you have protected yourself or your children. If we do not deal with these questions within the safe environment of family and congregation, many adults and children will simply assume we have no answers.

Comforting Those in Our Churches Who Are Doubting

The Gospels record an encounter between Jesus and a man whose son was afflicted by a demon. The man asked Jesus "if You can do anything, have compassion on us and help us" (Mark 9:22). We might be tempted to read this question as a reflection of the man's doubt in Jesus' abilities. The man certainly had his doubts! But what he was looking to Jesus for, it seems to me, was compassion and help.

Many Christians don't understand how our sinful nature still clings to us even after we have come to faith in Christ. Baptism is not a magical cure for doubt. In fact, true doubt is a precursor to stronger faith! But many Christians hide their doubts and concerns out of fear of being judged as less Christian because of them. Some Christians won't go to

> Don't stay alone in your doubts. Share them, and you will likely discover that others have answers to the matters that trouble you.

their pastors with questions for the same reason. These brothers and sisters in Christ may be silently crying out, "Would someone show me they care about the assault on my faith?"

Churches are not gyms for the spiritually fit but hospitals for those looking for spiritual cures. We are all simultaneously Daniels who are sure of their faith and Thomases who experience periods of doubt. It is good for congregations to develop a kind and generous attitude toward those struggling with their faith. Such struggles are not signs of a lack of belief but signs that belief is alive and fighting the devil, the world, and sinful human nature. The prophet Isaiah said of Jesus, the Messiah who was yet to come, that "a bruised reed He will not break, and a faintly burning wick He will not quench" (42:3). Congregations, which are the Body of Christ in the world, should act the same way.

Jesus told the father of the demon-possessed boy that "all things are possible for one who believes" (Mark 9:23). Many Christians at one point or another have made this man's words their own: "I believe; help my unbelief!" (v. 24). Let our congregations be places where the unbelief of the believers is helped and not increased.

Supporting Your Pastor

"Pastor spent four years in seminary. Surely he's already been taught everything he needs to know. Why do we need to pay for him to attend yet another conference?" You may have heard words similar to these. You may even have spoken them.

Certainly our seminary-trained pastors have a great theological foundation on which to build. They have studied the Scriptures in their original languages, considered the history of the Church through the ages, and studied the doctrines and dogmas that express our beliefs in Christ and in God. Many of the things pastors study in seminary have not changed for centuries. Some of them, especially the truths of the Scriptures, will never change.

Yet we live in a changing world. God's Word remains forever, but our culture and the ideas in it do not. Science is constantly changing. New theories are developed; old theories are refined or rejected. New arguments for and against the faith arise almost every day. These are the things of which a good pastor needs to remain aware. The Lord willing, they remember their theological training. But learning how to apply that theology to the changing world situation never stops. This is one reason why congregations should encourage their pastor to continue his education, especially in the areas of science and faith discussed in this book.

A second reason is for the pastor's own spiritual well-being. Consider this: You watch a television show, read a book, or check out a Web site that raises questions in your mind. You take those questions to your pastor, and rightly so. But so does everyone else in the congregation. You might be confronted with one issue in one week that leaves you puzzled. Your pastor may be confronted with half a dozen or more. Pastors are Christians too, and the constant barrage of questions can leave them with questions about their own faith. You turn to your pastor for answers. To whom does he turn? Attending conferences and seminars and reading books can give his faith the strengthening it needs. He, in turn, will be able to continue to strengthen you in your faith.

Final Thoughts

Satan's primary way of working in the world is separating people from God and one another. The devil is the great divider. Don't let him use your sinful nature to make you feel alone in your doubts. If you have a question about something, chances are others do too. Seek them out. When you come across something, whether it's a question or an answer, share it with your pastor. Most important, be prepared to comfort others who are also doubting. Jesus told Peter he would fall away from Him at His final trial. He said "I have prayed for you that your faith may not fail. And when you have turned again, strengthen your brothers" (Luke 22:32). When we come out of periods of doubt with our faith strengthened, we too ought to turn and comfort those around us.

> Speak out for your pastors in congregational meetings in support of their continuing education.

Key Points

● People have always had doubts; that is the nature of sin. Our Western scientific mental environment raises a unique set of doubts related to the origin and nature of life and creation.

- The best way to deal with doubts is to confront them.
- Congregations should intentionally seek to comfort, not condemn, those who have doubts and help resolve them.
- Pastors should be encouraged to continue their education, especially in the area of questions of science and faith, since this is such a significant issue in our time.

Discussion Questions

1. Do you remember a time when you had doubts about some aspect of the Christian faith? How did you resolve those doubts?

2. How might you offer constructive responses to a fellow Christian who expresses his or her doubts to you?

Action Items

1. Identify someone who can act as a resource person within your congregation on matters of science and faith. Let your pastor know who that person is.

2. Actively encourage your pastor to seek continuing education about issues of science and faith. Ask if there are particular topics he'd like to learn about, and see if you can help him find appropriate resources.

I have never lost my love of science. In fact, it has grown as I have realized that it is God Himself who gives us the intellect that allows us to appreciate His universe. At the same time, my humbleness has grown as well. God created us in His image, but that image was corrupted in the fall. Humanity is still, in many ways, like a child playing with adult tools and equipment. We can do great things that we could not do with the plastic toys in the nursery, but we can also do great damage. In the arena of science and technology, we have the potential for great good and for unspeakable evil.

My hope is that this book has helped you and perhaps your whole congregation to see science and technology in a more focused and scriptural light. I hope you have learned that research, in and of itself, is not something to fear. Research is conducted by humans, and what those humans believe about the world and our place in it impacts their conclusions, especially when it comes to things beyond our direct observation, things historical, and things that have not yet come to pass. Science is a powerful tool in understanding the things we can observe. But it is limited in what it reveals about things we cannot and will never be able to observe.

Paul wrote in 2 Corinthians that when it comes to understanding the Old Testament, there is a veil over the eyes of non-Christians. The minds of people are hardened to understanding even the plain words of prophecy Jesus used during

His earthly ministry. In Romans, he expanded that idea to all of creation, pointing out that sin prevents people from seeing the omnipotence, omniscience, and omnipresence of God. By nature, without God's Spirit in Christ, our hearts are hardened and our minds are closed to the knowledge of God. By nature, humans see the Bible as a fantastical book of contradictions. By nature, we believe nature says nothing about the existence of a Creator.

Christians know different because we are different. Those who have been baptized into Christ have received God's Spirit and can now see better, even if not perfectly. We can look at the Old Testament and see the history that proclaims a creative God of grace who desired to save us in Christ. We can study nature and see the fingerprints of a Creator within our cells and in the distant galaxies. Yet our old nature clings to us, raising doubts in our minds. God's Word, both on the written page and in the person of Jesus, is the antidote to those doubts. What we observe in the natural world will not conflict with what God has revealed to us through the prophets, apostles, evangelists, and psalmists. Those words sanctify us in the truth because they are the truth (John 17:17).

Let us not then be afraid to confront those with hardened hearts and darkened minds. Let us not be afraid to confront our own doubts. Dr. Caroline Crocker, a convert to Christianity who came to question the theory of evolution, was once told that it was okay to question the truth because if it is the truth, our questions cannot change it. Let us not be afraid to ask questions that will lead to better knowledge. With each answer we come to know Jesus, who is the truth, a little bit better. And knowing the Living Truth brings the greatest gift of all: freedom from sin, death, and the devil.